DEDICATION

This book is dedicate  Carolyn Randall, who
with me to wild and
friend Michelina Ceg
challenged me to finish this project strong.

—Jeff Eisele
October 2010

The Animas Valley stretches out north of Durango. PHOTO BY JEFF EISELE

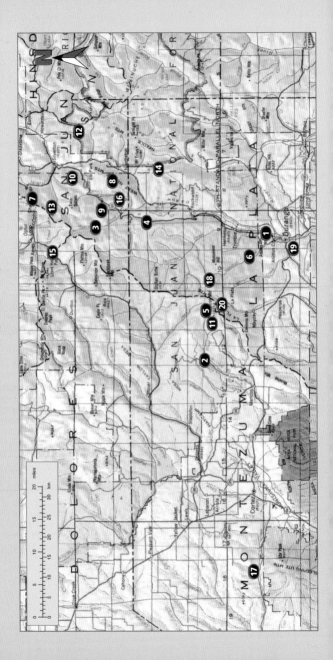

CONTENTS

ACKNOWLEDGMENTS

The Best Durango & Silverton Hikes is a volunteer project in the truest sense of the word and could not have been done without the knowledge, talents, energy, and commitment of all the contributors.

The reward? Yes, the writers and photographers get their names in print. Yes, the San Juan Group gets a small royalty for each book sold, but the contributors receive no personal compensation.

It's pretty simple, really. These are people who have a passion for hiking and climbing. Southwest Colorado is their home. They know its trails, and they're eager to share their knowledge and experience so that others can enjoy—and protect—these trails.

So it is that I extend my personal thanks to the contributors, in alphabetical order: Ken Beegles, Rob Blair, Dorothy Bregar, John Bregar, Diana Donnelly, Dianne Donovan, Mike Frisoni, Joe Griffith, Sandy Hoagland, Kerry Honsinger, Tom Hooten, Laszlo Szuecs, Bernadette Tuthill, Chip Tuthill, and Debra Van Winegarden. Thanks also to Péter Bodig, whose name doesn't appear anywhere else in the book but who contributed to the planning process from the very beginning and who wrote a trail description that later was substituted. You're all great company on the trail, and you're great to work with.

I also want to thank Series Editor John Gascoyne and CMC Publisher Alan Stark for their guidance, support, and patience with me in completing this project. It wasn't always easy, but it has been a rewarding and worthwhile experience, and I'm grateful for their confidence in me.

Thanks to CMC, for the knowledge and skills I've learned through its schools and programs; for the remarkable places it has taken me; for the opportunities to volunteer and share my talents with the club; and, most of all, for introducing me to some of the best and most loyal friends of my life. I've shared unmatchable experiences with them that I'll never forget.

JEFF EISELE

Foreword

The San Juan Group of The Colorado Mountain Club (CMC) welcomes you to Durango and Southwest Colorado.

Group members' initial challenge in producing this book was perhaps the hardest—selecting the "best" 20 hikes in a region encompassing hundreds of trails and seemingly limitless beauty. The list started long. It took several rounds of cuts—and, at times, some passionate debate—before we arrived at the hikes in this book.

The hikes cover a region extending from the mesa country of the high desert west of Cortez, to Durango, and north to Silverton and beyond. Most are in the La Plata Mountains west of Durango and the San Juan Mountains to the north. Destinations include the summits of prominent local mountain landmarks in Durango; cliff dwellings and ruins of the ancient Anasazi people; the remains of once-booming mining operations; trails along streams, through forests, leading to alpine lakes; and off-trail ascents to summits over 13,000 feet. They encompass all ability levels, including the handicapped-accessible Big Al Trail—there's something for everyone, from the novice visitor to experienced Coloradans.

There are hazards. Chief among them, especially for out-of-state visitors, are altitude sickness, dehydration, and hypothermia. Take time to acclimatize, carry plenty of water, and pace yourself. Bring clothing to protect yourself from inclement weather, which can change in a matter of minutes. Wind, rain, hail, or snow can occur almost any time at high elevation. Lightning above timberline is not a pleasant experience. Plan ahead, start early, and return before storms materialize.

Above all, enjoy yourself and help protect this pristine environment. It's fragile and easily damaged by human encroachment. Help preserve it now and for future generations by practicing Leave No Trace principles (see page 97).

JEFF EISELE, *author, group member, trip leader*
San Juan Group, The Colorado Mountain Club

Castle Rock from near the trailhead at Needles Country Square.

INTRODUCTION

How to Use This Book

Each trail description includes four sections:

► **Basic data**, including:
  - **Maps:** Trails Illustrated, USGS, and any other relevant maps of the area
  - **Elevation gain**
  - **Rating:** On a 5-point scale (Easy; Easy–Moderate; Moderate; Moderate–Difficult; Difficult)
  - **Round-trip distance**
  - **Round-trip time**
  - **Nearest landmark**.

► **COMMENT:** A general description of the hike, its features and highlights, and what the hiker may encounter.

► **GETTING THERE:** detailed directions to the trailhead.

► **THE ROUTE:** a description from trailhead to the destination, and back, and any optional extensions.

Color photographs and a full-color topographic map accompany each hike. While these maps may be sufficient in helping you navigate to your destination, the maps identified in the data at the top of each hike generally will provide more detail and include a much wider surrounding area.

A Note About Ratings

Novice hikers will have a number of hikes rated "Easy" and "Easy–Moderate" to choose from in this book, but I encourage you also to consider shortening the higher-rated hikes to make them easier. In many cases, you can enjoy much of what a route has to offer without going to the end of the described hike, and keep it within your abilities. For example, the hike on the Lime Mesa Trail to Mountain View Crest (page 68) is rated as

"Moderate–Difficult" because of the distance (9–10 miles) and altitude (11,250–12,998 feet). The trail, however, is well defined, with no exposure along the entire route. If you make it an 8-mile round trip, turning around 1–2 miles before Overlook Point, you'll still enjoy much of what the hike has to offer in a shorter period of time and with less exertion.

Colorado Weather and Safety

Thunderstorms are common in Southwest Colorado in summer, especially during the "monsoon" season in July and August, and are not unusual in spring and fall, as well. The typical pattern is clear mornings with clouds and potential storms building by midday, and often becoming threatening in the afternoon. That's why perhaps the best advice is to get an early start, planning to reach your destination by late morning and being on your way back to the trailhead by noon. This is especially critical for high-altitude destinations above timberline. You do not want to get caught in an electrical storm above timberline.

Always carry extra clothing, rain gear, and other essential items you might need to survive in case of unexpected circumstances. For more details, see the section in this book titled "The Ten Essentials System" on page 13.

Search and Rescue Card

Colorado has a Search and Rescue Fund to help local agencies cover the costs of search-and-rescue operations. Money for the fund is provided by a surcharge on hunting and fishing licenses and vessel, snowmobile, and off-highway vehicle registrations. People who don't have one of those licenses, registrations, or a CORSAR (Colorado Outdoor Recreation Search and Rescue) card could be billed for some expenses related to a search and rescue, which can be extensive. A CORSAR card can be purchased at a cost of $3 for an annual card or $12 for a five-year card. You can purchase a CORSAR card from outdoor,

The intersection of the Engineer Mountain and Pass Creek trails in the meadows above timberline.

recreation, and sporting goods retailers and organizations throughout the state or online at https://dola.colorado .gov/dlg/fa/sar/sar_purchase.html.

A sign marks the southern terminus of the Colorado Trail, the start of the hike to Gudy's Rest.

PHOTO BY LASZLO SZUECS

THE TEN ESSENTIALS SYSTEM

The Colorado Mountain Club (CMC) is the author and publisher of this pack guide. Since 1912, the CMC has promoted wilderness safety awareness and has distilled the essential safety items down to a list known as "The Ten Essentials." We present it here in a "systems" approach. Carrying the items from this list that are appropriate for the location, mileage, and elevation of your hike will help you be fully prepared for every trip and able to survive the unexpected emergency.

1. **Insulation.** Carry enough extra clothing to stay dry and protected from the wind and rain, no matter what. Wool or synthetic insulating layers under a windproof, water-resistant shell with a hood is a good system. Be sure to include a warm hat, as 70 percent of the body's heat escapes from the head. Also, consider gloves and wind pants. Avoid cotton, which is cold when wet, even from sweat.

2. **Hydration.** Carry at least 2 quarts of water on any hike. For longer hikes, carry more water or a water-purification system such as tablets or a filter. Drink water before the hike and have a reserve bottle in the car for after the hike. If you don't drink until you're thirsty, you've waited too long.

3. **Nutrition.** Eat a good breakfast and pack a healthy lunch. Carry extra food such as trail mix or energy bars.

4. **Emergency shelter.** Carry something that could shelter you from wind and rain overnight. The simplest shelter could be a large plastic leaf bag. Better yet would be a space blanket with nylon cords tied to the corners. A heavier and more-expensive solution is a commercial bivouac sack. Also, carry a piece of foam insulation to sit on, if your pack doesn't have one inside it already.

5. **Fire.** At a minimum, carry waterproof matches. Also carry a lighter, a fire ribbon, magnesium shavings, or another fire-starting device. Carry kindling, such as commercial fire-starter sticks, wadded paper, steel wool, or cotton dryer lint or cotton balls impregnated with Vaseline. Dry pine needles or tree sap can work in a pinch. Practice starting fires in cold, wet, and windy conditions. *However, consider well the appropriateness of fire for survival in a fire-sensitive area versus simply hiking out.*

6. **Sun protection.** Use sunblock on all exposed skin and lip balm on the lips, even on cloudy days. Wear sunglasses and a wide-brimmed hat.

7. **Navigation.** Familiarize yourself with the general direction, elevation, landmarks, and surrounding terrain of the hike. Carry and know how to use a map and compass. GPS units are no substitute for map-and-compass knowledge, but they can be useful to find specific points in darkness or in whiteout conditions.

8. **Illumination.** A flashlight with extra batteries and an extra bulb is a minimum. An extra flashlight is even better. One of them should be a headlamp to free the hands for other tasks. Test each flashlight and put in fresh batteries before the hike.

9. **First-aid kit.** Outfit your first-aid kit with germicidal soap or ointment, bandages, first-aid tape, anti-inflammatory pain tablets, moleskin for blisters, a bandana, an ace bandage, eyewash, latex gloves, and a mouth-to-mouth barrier in case you need to care for someone else. Add special medications if you or your companions have special needs: glucose tablets for diabetes, an EpiPen for extreme insect allergies, or an inhaler for asthma.

10. **Emergency tools and supplies.** Carry a knife, repair tape, a length of nylon cord, a whistle, a signal mirror, a small trowel, toilet paper, and a Ziploc bag for used toilet paper.

Mount Wilson, center, and Gladstone Peak tower over the Lizard Head Trail.

Also consider a small pair of scissors for cutting moleskin and small pliers. Many of the above are combined in nifty multi-tools.

A NOTE ON HYPOTHERMIA

Hypothermia (exposure) is the most immediate danger in the outdoors. If you get wet, can't get dry, and can't get out of the wind, a refrigeration system is at work that will lower your body temperature until you die. People have died in as little as an hour in above-freezing conditions. One of the first casualties of exposure is rational thought, and with it goes the ability of the victim to save himself or herself by clear thinking. If you feel profoundly cold, deal with it immediately. Better yet, be prepared:

- Windproof and waterproof clothing and a hat are your walls and roof.
- Adequate hydration is your heat circulator. It keeps your blood thin and flowing well.
- Adequate nutrition is the fire in your furnace.

1. Animas Mountain Trail

BY ROB BLAIR

MAPS	Trails Illustrated, Durango/Cortez, Number 144 USGS, Durango East 7.5 minute; Durango West 7.5 minute Latitude 40, Durango Trails
ELEVATION GAIN	1,480 feet
RATING	Easy
ROUND-TRIP DISTANCE	6.2 miles
ROUND-TRIP TIME	3–4.5 hours
NEAREST LANDMARK	Intersection of Main Avenue and 32nd Street in Durango

COMMENT: Animas Mountain is a prominent peak north of Durango, rising to an altitude of 8,161 feet. The peak is officially named Animas City Mountain, after the town that once was at its base in the present-day area of north Durango. Indeed, it's called Animas City Mountain on USGS topo maps and on the map in this pack guide. Locals, however, generally refer to it as Animas Mountain.

The loop provides stunning views from the east rim of the lower Animas River Valley. This glacially eroded valley is host to a textbook meandering river with cut-off abandoned channels and oxbow lakes. The trail follows the tilted surface of the resistant Dakota sandstone, whose layers dip 10 degrees to the southwest. Directly east near the skyline, you can see the whitish scar left from a 1998 rockfall from the Dakota rim rock.

If your timing is right, early in the morning or late afternoon, you can hear and see a Durango & Silverton Narrow Gauge Railroad steam engine chugging its way along the valley floor. The whistle echoes between the steep valley walls the same way it did in the late 1800s.

Animas Mountain dominates the northwestern edge of Durango.

To the north, the summit affords views of Precambrian gneisses comprising the highest peaks along the skyline. The Falls Creek hidden valley also can be seen to the north; its origin is still a mystery. What role did glaciations play? Was it an old, abandoned channel of Hermosa Creek farther north?

The climb from the parking lot to the rim passes through piñon/juniper woodland, and once on the Dakota rim rock, the vegetation is dominated by ponderosa pine with a Gambel oak understory.

The trail loop is on Bureau of Land Management land and has been designated as elk habitat and winter-feeding range. For this reason, the trail is closed to human travel from Dec. 1 to April 15. During the open months, horses, mountain bikers, runners, and hikers use the trail. In years of heavy early-season snowfall, snowshoers also use it before the December closure.

GETTING THERE: From the intersection of Main Avenue and 32nd Street, go west on 32nd Street, then turn north on West Fourth Avenue (the one-way sign does not apply when

A view from the summit of Falls Creek Valley, center, and Animas Valley, right, with the San Juans in the distance.   PHOTO BY ROB BLAIR

turning right). Follow this street until it ends at a parking area. A trailhead sign identifies the start.

THE ROUTE: From the trailhead sign, follow the path as it zigzags its way above the rimrock—this guide assumes you are going in a counterclockwise direction. There are at least two spur trails off to the west in the first half-mile; stay to the right. In fact, during the ascent, "when in doubt, go right" will keep you on the main trail. As you will see, part of the trail at times follows old logging roads. Along the way, the east-side portion of the trail often approaches the rim, affording several panoramic views of Durango, the Animas River Valley, and the San Juan Mountains.

The summit at the north end of the mountain—not marked and no register—is thick with Gambel oak. From here, there is a clear view of the Falls Creek Valley directly below to the north, as well as the La Plata Mountains to the west.

You can retrace your ascent route for the return or follow the western trail that loops back to the start. To return to the parking lot, take a hard left turn (east) at a power utility pole where the trail levels out.

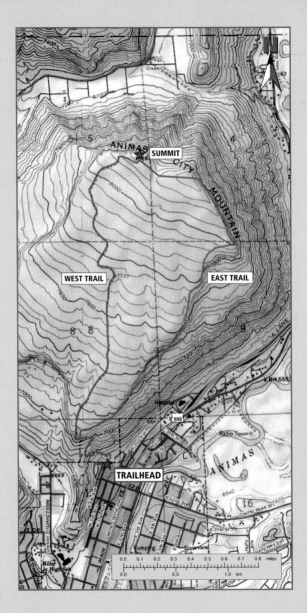

2. Big Al Trail and West Mancos River Loop

BY BERNADETTE TUTHILL

MAPS	Trails Illustrated, Durango/Cortez, Number 144
	USGS, Rampart Hills 7.5 minute
	Latitude 40, Durango Trails
ELEVATION GAIN	80 feet; 750 feet
RATING	Easy; easy–moderate
ROUND-TRIP DISTANCE	0.8 mile; 3.8 miles
ROUND-TRIP TIME	0.5–1 hour; 3–4 hours
NEAREST LANDMARK	Transfer Campground

COMMENT: The Big Al Trail and West Mancos River Loop are part of the Transfer Recreation Area, which includes many hiking trails, a campground, and picnic areas. The areas are accessible only spring through fall.

The Big Al Trail is a barrier-free, surfaced gravel trail leading to a deck overlooking West Mancos Canyon, with spectacular views of the La Plata Mountains. The trail was named for Al Lorentzen, a Forest Service employee who was disabled by a falling tree while fighting a fire near Yellowstone in 1988. This trail is suitable for all ages and abilities and is dedicated to "all people who have experienced a disability." There are interpretive signs along the way and benches every few hundred feet.

The West Mancos River Loop is a short hike on sections of four trails. It takes you along the West Mancos Canyon rim, with more breathtaking views of the La Platas, then drops below the rim for an up-and-down ramble along the West Mancos River, before an ascent back to the rim.

GETTING THERE: From Durango, go west on U.S. 160 for 27 miles, to the junction with Colorado 184 in Mancos. Take 184 north

Hikers are treated to many panoramic views of Hesperus Mountain, the highest peak in the La Plata Range, along the Big Al Trail and West Mancos River Loop.

PHOTO BY BERNADETTE TUTHILL

0.3 mile and turn onto Montezuma County Road 42, at a sign for Mancos State Park and Jackson Lake. Follow this road 10 miles to a turnoff to the Transfer Campground on the right. Go 0.2 mile, passing the West Mancos Overlook on your right, to the campground entrance and trailhead parking on the left.

THE ROUTES: The Big Al Trail starts across the road from the parking area, on the left side of a signboard. This easy walking trail will lead you to a large viewing platform with dramatic views. Spend some time relaxing and taking in the scenery.

The West Mancos Creek Loop begins on the Rim Trail, at a signboard at the West Mancos Overlook—which you passed driving into the parking area. Here is another stunning view of the La Platas and Hesperus Mountain, one of the sacred mountains of the Navajo people. Follow the Rim Trail for 1 mile, passing through cattle gates after 0.2 and 0.9 miles.

Alpine lupines along the gentle and wide Big Al Trail.   PHOTO BY JEFF EISELE

Secure the gates after passing through. This brings you to a junction with the Box Canyon Trail.

Continue the loop in a counterclockwise direction. The Box Canyon Trail switchbacks down to West Mancos Creek, through groves of aspen and ponderosa pine. After 1.75 miles from the trailhead, you come to a double-track road, which is the combined West Mancos Creek and Transfer trails. Turn left and come to a gated water-control facility. The trail continues on the left, with many short, sometimes steep, ups and downs as it follows the contours of the canyon wall. About a mile into your hike along the creek, you will come to a large boulder extending into the river. This is a great place to take a break and listen to the water in spring, or take a cool dip in summer when the water is not flowing too fast.

After another 0.3 mile, the trail begins its ascent from the creek. After 3.4 miles from the trailhead, you come to a junction. The West Mancos Trail branches off to the right; bear left here, continuing your counterclockwise route to complete the loop and return to the Transfer Trailhead, next to the parking area. Look behind you occasionally to catch more stunning views of Hesperus Mountain.

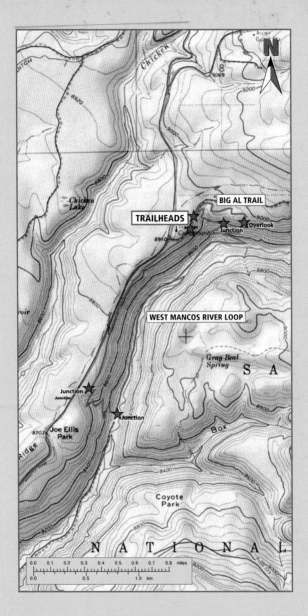

3. Cascade Creek Trail

BY JOE GRIFFITH AND DIANNE DONOVAN

MAPS	Trails Illustrated, Durango/Cortez, Number 144 (includes beginning of the trail) USGS, Engineer Mountain 7.5 minute Latitude 40, Durango Trails
ELEVATION GAIN	700 feet
RATING	Easy–moderate
ROUND-TRIP DISTANCE	7 miles
ROUND-TRIP TIME	3–5 hours
NEAREST LANDMARK	Durango Mountain Resort

COMMENT: There are two trails ascending Cascade Creek, on opposite sides of the creek. The west side trail, unlike the one on the east side, ascends through beautiful old woods. This trail stays close enough to the creek to continually lull you with the sound of water cascading over rocks and ledges. There are several creek crossings, so this hike is best done after the spring runoff; July through October are optimal hiking months. You can bring sandals and a small towel for the creek crossings. In winter, the trail is suitable for crosscountry skiing and snowshoeing, with at least a 2-foot snow cover.

The trail begins at 8,900 feet elevation and ascends to 9,600 feet. Dogs must be on a leash and under control.

GETTING THERE: From U.S. 550 and 32nd Street in Durango, drive 27 miles north on U.S. 550. Pass Durango Mountain Resort and Cascade Village, and immediately after a hairpin turn over Cascade Creek, turn left at the signed Forest Service road. You can park here or drive 0.75 mile on this gravel road to a small parking lot on the left, just before the road rises and crosses a flume.

THE ROUTE: The hike begins on the east side of the creek. Follow the rough road over the flume, passing a group of occupied

A view of Cascade Creek from the trail.

PHOTO BY JOE GRIFFITH

cabins. This is the site of the old Yeager Lumber Mill. In 1.0 mile, there is a gate beyond which motor travel is forbidden. Continue through the gate. The trail takes a right turn and passes an abandoned cabin, crosses a broad, shallow creek area (with very heavy gravel deposits) and continues 0.25 mile to an intersection. The right fork is the trail going up the east side. Take the fork to the left and then go sharply left. You will come to a wide, shallow, and rocky crossing of Cascade Creek.

Once across the creek, take the trail to the right (north). After passing a sign on the left (Camp Creek), the trail gets a bit rocky for 0.25 mile before settling into a pleasant single track. From here, the trail passes through old woods, staying close to the creek. The trail crosses Pando Creek after 2 miles, continues on to cross EZ Creek and, after crossing a steep meadow, goes on for a short distance before crossing Graysill Creek.

The Cascade Creek headwaters from the end of the hike. PHOTO BY JOE GRIFFITH

Immediately after Graysill Creek, the trail climbs moderately through a wooded area. As you climb, look for an indistinct spur trail on the right that leads to a view of a pretty waterfall on Cascade Creek.

Back on the trail, you will climb a bit more, then pass through a deadfall area and emerge into a nice camping spot 3.5 miles from the trailhead. This is a good place to end your hike. As you look up the creek to the north, you will see the mountain cirque that forms the headwaters of Cascade Creek.

At this spot, the Graysill connector trail turns left and goes uphill (west) to cross the Cascade Divide Road. Another trail turns slightly right and descends to a crossing of Cascade Creek. If you want to continue, cross the creek and find the trail in the meadow. Following it north, you will pass a series of steps, each 10 to 15 feet high. At each of these steps there is a beautiful waterfall on Cascade Creek. Eventually—after some confusing blowdown areas, overgrown meadows, and another creek crossing—the trail joins the Colorado Trail just west of where it crosses Cascade Creek. Retrace your steps to return to the trailhead.

TRAILHEAD

N

| 0.0 | 0.5 | 1.0 miles |
| 0.0 | 0.5 | 1.0 | 1.5 km |

4. Castle Rock

BY SANDY HOAGLAND

MAPS	Trails Illustrated, Durango/Cortez, Number 144
	USGS, Electra Lake 7.5 minute
	Latitude 40, Durango Trails
ELEVATION GAIN	1,600 feet
RATING	Moderate
ROUND-TRIP DISTANCE	5.5 miles
ROUND-TRIP TIME	3–4 hours
NEAREST LANDMARK	Needles Country Square

COMMENT: Castle Rock is a prominent rock outcropping in the Hermosa cliffs, high above U.S. 550 north of Durango. The trail to this overlook travels through aspen, spruce, and pine forests, as well as a meadow. It culminates at a fine viewpoint 1,600 feet above the starting point. Views extend north and east into the San Juan Mountains, as well as south down the Animas Valley. In late spring and summer you may see strawberries, violets, and wild iris along the trail, while the aspen will be radiant in the fall. Hunters may also use this trail in the fall, so you will want to wear blaze orange during hunting season. This also is a nice area for snowshoeing in winter. The snow trail may be hard to follow if no one has packed it recently; there are no trail blazes on the trees.

GETTING THERE: From 32nd Street in Durango, go 22 miles north on U.S. 550 to Needles Country Square, a center with a gas station, grocery and outdoor stores, and corral, on the left (west) side of the highway. There is a parking area near the trailhead, at the south end of the square and near the east end of the corral. Take care not to park in designated customer spaces.

THE ROUTE: The approach to Castle Rock is over the Elbert Creek Trail and begins at the east end of the corral south of the

A hiker stands on top of Castle Rock.

PHOTO BY SANDY HOAGLAND

Needles Country Square. There is a sign for Elbert Creek Trail, and a marker indicates the trail is open to hikers, bikers, and equestrians. Go through either side of the corral, closing the gates as you go. At first, the trail is fenced as it travels alongside private property. After about .25 mile, you will cross Elbert Creek—across some downed trees; there may be a rope line available for added support. Soon after, switchbacks begin through the aspen as the trail ascends. You will soon have a view of Electra Lake in the valley below.

Above the switchbacks, the trail travels through a spruce forest. Elbert Creek can still be heard, although at this point the trail has risen away from it. Approximately 1.8 miles from the trailhead, there is a National Forest cabin at the edge of a

Twilight Peak in winter snow from Castle Rock.   PHOTO BY JEFF EISELE

meadow. Although locked, the cabin has emergency supplies for the stranded traveler. A few hundred yards beyond the cabin, 2 miles from the trailhead, is the junction with the trail to Castle Rock on the right. The junction is marked only with a post, but it should be easy to locate. The trail to Castle Rock ascends the slope north of the cabin and soon enters a drainage, which often holds snow into late spring.

Soon the trail moves out of the east side of the drainage and climbs some more before emerging on top of the cliff band. Continue on the trail along the cliff top until you can look straight down on the highway and Needles Country Square. This is your destination, and it provides a lovely place to relax, enjoy the views, and have a snack. Twilight Peak towers across the valley with high peaks of the Weminuche Wilderness beyond. Return by retracing your steps to the trailhead.

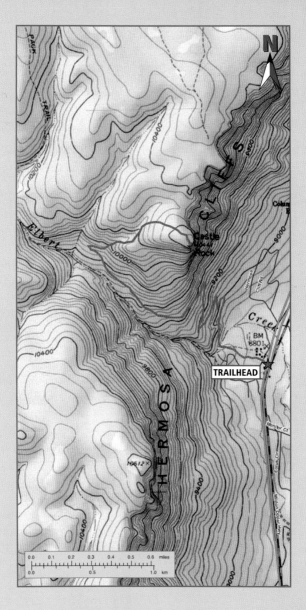

5. Centennial Peak

BY SANDY HOAGLAND

MAPS	Trails Illustrated, Durango/Cortez, Number 144 USGS, La Plata 7.5 minute Latitude 40, Durango Trails
ELEVATION GAIN	2,160 feet
RATING	Moderate
ROUND-TRIP DISTANCE	5 miles (8 miles from spur road intersection)
ROUND-TRIP TIME	3.5–4.5 hours (5–6 hours from spur road intersection)
NEAREST LANDMARK	Town of Mancos

COMMENT: Centennial Peak is an enjoyable day hike on the west side of the La Plata Mountain Range, with stunning views of much of the San Juan Mountains. The hike to the saddle at Sharkstooth Pass will reward you with an abundance of wildflowers in July and August, both in the forest and in the alpine meadow above. At the saddle, the mountain views of nearby Sharkstooth Peak, Hesperus Mountain (the highest peak in the La Plata Range), and jagged Lavender Peak are impressive. An additional climb of 1,150 feet, and 0.7 mile, will bring you to the 13,062-foot summit of Centennial Peak, with up-close views of Lavender Peak.

GETTING THERE: From Durango, go west on U.S. 160 for 27 miles to the junction with Colorado 184 in Mancos. From here, it is 19.8 miles to your driving destination—the Sharkstooth trailhead, mostly on good paved or gravel roads. Mark from this point. Take 184 north 0.3 mile and turn right onto Montezuma County Road 42 at a sign for Mancos State Park and Jackson Lake. At mile 5.5 you enter the San Juan National Forest and the road becomes Forest Service Road 561. The Transfer Campground is at mile 10.0. There are additional

Centennial and Lavender peaks from Sharkstooth Peak's summit.

PHOTO BY SANDY HOAGLAND

roadside camping opportunities farther along the road, except at the trailhead, where camping is prohibited. At mile 12.0, turn right onto FS 350 (Spruce Mill Road). A few roads will branch off, but stay on FS 350 until mile 18.3, veering right on a spur road marked by a sign for Twin Lakes and Sharkstooth Trailhead. A high-clearance, four-wheel-drive vehicle is recommended beyond this point. Follow this road for 1.5 miles to the trailhead.

THE ROUTE: There are two trailheads at this parking area. The Sharkstooth Trail, which heads east through spruce and fir forest, is the one that leads to Centennial Peak. The West Mancos Trail heads south and eventually turns opposite of the intended direction, so do not take this trail.

About halfway up to the saddle between Sharkstooth and Centennial peaks, the trail diverges. The main trail stays to the

Sharkstooth, left, and Centennial peaks, as they appear from the west.
PHOTO BY SANDY HOAGLAND

right, but you can also take the left fork, which is not much longer and which travels past the ruins of the Williams Mine. There are some informative signs about this mine, which was most recently active in 1988. The mine trail rejoins the Sharkstooth Trail above the mine, where it climbs more before arriving at a beautiful alpine meadow. During summer months, this meadow is home to a wonderful array of wildflowers.

The high point of the Sharkstooth Trail is at the top of the Sharkstooth-Centennial saddle, 1.8 miles from the trailhead. It is marked with a sign at 11,936 feet. The Sharkstooth Trail continues down the other side of the pass, but that is not the goal here—instead, turn south toward Centennial Peak and climb the ridge in front of you.

There is a trail, which may be intermittent, on the west side of the ridge. Once you climb above the first steep part, there is a gentler, grassy slope where the trail may be hard to follow. Just continue up the grassy slope and stay just west of the ridge as you get into the talus. There is a fairly good trail through the talus leading to the summit. Your efforts will be rewarded with fine views of the Needle Mountains to the northeast, the San Miguel Mountains to the north, the Abajo Mountains in Utah to the west, and Sleeping Ute Mountain to the southwest. Retrace your steps to return to the trailhead.

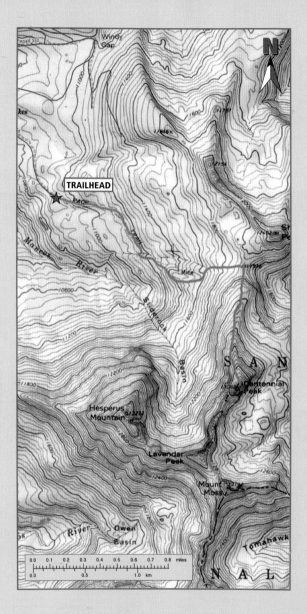

6. Colorado Trail—Gudy's Rest

BY LASZLO SZUECS

MAPS	Trails Illustrated, Durango/Cortez, Number 144
	USGS, Durango West 7.5 minute
	Latitude 40, Durango Trails
	Single Track Maps, Durango
ELEVATION GAIN	900 feet (700 feet from upper trailhead)
RATING	Moderate (easy from upper trailhead)
ROUND-TRIP DISTANCE	6 miles (4 miles from upper trailhead)
ROUND-TRIP TIME	3.5 hours (2.5 hours from upper trailhead)
NEAREST LANDMARK	Main Avenue and 25th Street in Durango

COMMENT: A locals' favorite, the hike to Gudy's Rest covers the first 3 miles of the Colorado Trail, whose other end is 480 miles away, on the outskirts of Denver. Gudy's Rest is a scenic viewpoint, named after Gudy Gaskill, the chief driving force behind construction of the Colorado Trail, which took place between 1973 and 1987.

Best times to hike the trail are in the spring (late April or early May) and fall (late September through October). The turning leaves in October make the hike especially spectacular. You may encounter bikers on the trail; they usually give you a friendly "thank you" for stepping aside to let them pass. During the summer months, an early start is advised in order to avoid the midday heat.

In the winter, the trail is normally snow-covered. The first 2 miles typically are packed by hikers and also can be icy in spots. Beyond that, you may need snowshoes.

GETTING THERE: From downtown Durango, drive north on Main Avenue to 25th Street and turn left; 25th Street is soon called Junction Street, then Junction Creek Road (County Road 204). At 2.9 miles from Main Avenue, a road will branch off to the right (to Falls Creek), but you will continue straight,

A hiker takes in the panorama from Gudy's Rest.   PHOTO BY LASZLO SZUECS

following the sign to the Colorado Trail. At 3.5 miles from
Main Avenue, the pavement will end at the National Forest
boundary; turn left into the lower trailhead parking area.
There are pit toilets here. If you choose to start at the upper
trailhead, continue to drive another mile on the Forest
Service road, to a hairpin curve on the right, and park in the
small, designated parking area.

THE ROUTE: The first mile from the lower trailhead follows
Junction Creek very closely on its north side, at the bottom of
a canyon. It is shaded and can be cool even in summer. After
1.0 mile, the trail goes past the upper trailhead and continues
about 150 feet above the creek bed. The deciduous trees near
the creek in this area provide spectacular autumn color.

About 0.5 mile past the upper trailhead, look for a large,
reddish cliff, high above the canyon floor, with a large gray hole
where a chunk of the reddish rock broke off some time in the
past. Gudy's Rest is at the right end of the top of this cliff.

A winter view of Perins Peak from Gudy's Rest. PHOTO BY JEFF EISELE

At 1.0 mile past the upper trailhead, the trail crosses over to the south side of Junction Creek on a sturdy wooden bridge. Over the last mile of the hike, you'll encounter several switchbacks as the trail gently gains elevation over the canyon floor. The forest consists mainly of ponderosa pine. At some of the switchbacks, you can look up and see the reddish cliffs where Gudy's Rest is located. You will finally arrive at your destination and can relax on a wooden bench and take in the view. In the valley to the east, you will see the Fort Lewis College campus, on the flat mesa above Durango. The prominent mesa to the southeast is Perins Peak. Retrace your steps to return to the trailhead.

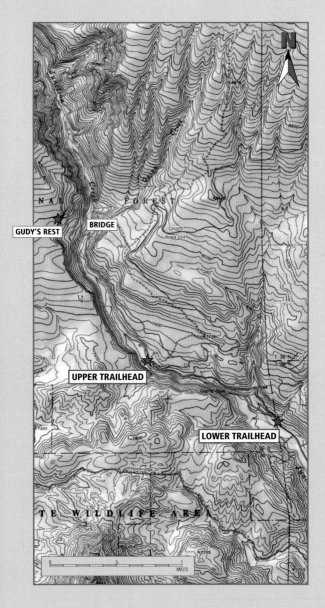

GUDY'S REST

BRIDGE

UPPER TRAILHEAD

LOWER TRAILHEAD

7. Columbine Lake Trail

BY JEFF EISELE

MAPS	Trails Illustrated, Telluride/Silverton/Ouray/Lake City, Number 141 USGS, Ophir/Silverton 7.5 minute Latitude 40, Telluride/Silverton/Ouray
ELEVATION GAIN	2,460 feet (2,820 feet from bridge parking area)
RATING	Moderate
ROUND-TRIP DISTANCE	8.3 miles (9.9 miles from bridge parking area)
ROUND-TRIP TIME	4.5–6.5 hours (add 1 hour from bridge parking area)
NEAREST LANDMARK	Town of Silverton

COMMENT: This unmarked trail is a well-kept secret locally and gets little use, but it is in good condition and well defined almost all of the way to Columbine Lake. It's a moderately steep climb above timberline that eases to a delightful tundra walk with gradual ascents over the last 1.5 miles to the lake. The wildflower show in summer is spectacular. The destination is a large, high alpine lake surrounded by several peaks over 13,000 feet elevation.

GETTING THERE: From 32nd Street in Durango, drive 46 miles north on U.S. 550 to Silverton. Continue on 550 for 5 miles and turn left on the Ophir Pass Road. Follow this road a short distance as it crosses a bridge over Mineral Creek, curves left, and begins ascending. Turn right on the first unmarked road. This is Forest Service Road 820, which is confirmed by signage a short distance up the road. Take this road 0.7 mile to the unmarked trailhead. There is room for only a couple of vehicles at a pullout about 100 feet south of the trailhead. If this is occupied, there are other pullouts nearby, or you can park in a spacious area next to the bridge over Mineral Creek. This last option, however, will add 1.6 miles to your hike.

The deep turquoise of Columbine Lake, surrounded by magnificent thirteeners.   PHOTO BY JEFF EISELE

THE ROUTE: Starting at 10,100 feet, the trail angles above the road to the right, then begins a series of switchbacks over the first 1.3 miles through the forest, up a steep, east-facing mountainside. This brings you to timberline and your first views of the high peaks you're heading toward. None of them except Lookout Peak has an official name, but many of them rise above 13,000 feet.

With the switchbacks behind you, and now with an open view to the west, continue through some steep sections over the next 1.2 miles, toward an impressive mountain. It has three summits, two of them over 13,000 feet. You're now at 12,450 feet, and the trail swings to the north to skirt around the mountain. You've come a little over half of the one-way distance, and now the grade eases as you move into beautiful tundra carpeted in grass and wildflowers. It will be like this the rest of the way until just before you reach the lake.

Over the next 0.6 mile, the trail gradually turns back to the west. The wide, deep chasm of Mill Creek gradually reveals

Above timberline, the trail ascends toward an impressive mountain, with two high points over 13,000 feet.

PHOTO BY JEFF EISELE

itself below you to the north, with another impressive, broad, and unnamed thirteener above it, and Lookout Peak (13,661 feet)—rising just above your destination to the west—comes into view for the first time.

The trail continues west for another 0.75 mile, then turns south and follows an outlet stream up to the lake at 12,685 feet. Lookout Peak and several other thirteeners surround the stunning, deep-turquoise-colored lake on three sides. Return to the trailhead by retracing your path.

TRAILHEAD

8. Crater Lake Trail

BY JOE GRIFFITH AND DIANNE DONOVAN

MAPS	Trails Illustrated, Weminuche Wilderness, Number 140
	USGS, Snowdon Peak 7.5 minute
	Latitude 40, Durango Trails
ELEVATION GAIN	1,300 feet
RATING	Moderate
ROUND-TRIP DISTANCE	11 miles
ROUND-TRIP TIME	5–8 hours
NEAREST LANDMARK	Andrews Lake

COMMENT: This trail is a 50-minute drive from Durango, to the trailhead at Andrews Lake. Your hike begins at 10,750 feet and reaches 11,700 feet before it descends to Crater Lake. The trail offers spectacular views of the San Juan Mountains and is inspiring, whether you make it short or long.

The full hike to Crater Lake can be done round-trip in one day by serious hikers, or it can be an overnight backpacking adventure. There is much to see around Crater Lake, and a two-night stay with a day to explore the area is a good option.

Winter will see about 2 feet of snow in the area, and you can crosscountry ski around Andrews Lake and enjoy backcountry skiing and snowshoeing on the trail. Dogs must be on leash and under control.

GETTING THERE: From Durango, drive 39 miles north on U.S. 550, over Coal Bank Pass. One mile before reaching Molas Pass, turn right onto the Andrews Lake Road. This paved road ends in less than 1 mile, at a large parking area with toilet facilities next to Andrews Lake.

THE ROUTE: From the parking lot, walk past the toilets across the bridge over the outlet of Andrews Lake. Bear uphill to the right to a Forest Service sign and the Crater Lake Trail

Snowdon Peak looms over Snowdon Meadow.   PHOTO BY JOE GRIFFITH

register. The elevation here is about 10,800 feet.

The trail goes east for 0.1 mile, then turns right and begins switchbacking up, with spectacular views to the west. At the ridge top (11,200 feet) there are excellent views of Mount Snowdon and the meadows below. (If you want a shorter hike, this is a good turnaround point. Or, you could explore Snowdon Meadow and the approach to Snowdon Peak. To do that, follow the trail that descends east from the ridge, bearing slightly left. You can see the trail from the ridgeline, as it crosses the meadow and enters the Weminuche Wilderness.)

The Crater Lake Trail continues over the ridgeline, slabs down gently to the right (south), passes a pond, and continues gently downhill past outcroppings of Molas limestone and then enters the woods. A zigzag path leads out of the woods and across a small stream and then climbs steeply over a small hill, to a soggy spot with the Weminuche Wilderness sign just beyond.

Looking west from Crater Lake—the San Juans, with Twin Sisters at left.

PHOTO BY JOE GRIFFITH

The trail then gets a bit rougher, with occasional bogs and rocky sections. It slabs up the side of a hill, with great views, crests in the woods at 11,400 feet, and then descends on zigzags to cross Three Lakes Creek—a step-over crossing. From here to Crater Lake, the trail is gently rolling, with very good views to the south and west.

In 1 mile more, there is an unmarked trail to the left; ignore this. The main trail continues around open fields, crosses several brooks, goes through a blowdown area at 11,700 feet (where hardworking crews have hewed out the trail), and then comes to an overlook of a swampy area. Follow the trail down and to the right and shortly you will arrive at Crater Lake. There are campsites around the area—with views of the West Needles Mountains (also known as the Twilights). If you choose to camp there, be prepared for a robust mosquito population. Retrace your steps for the return trip.

TRAILHEAD

9. Engineer Mountain

BY KEN BEEGLES

MAPS	Trails Illustrated, Telluride/ Silverton/ Ouray/Lake City, Number 141 USGS, Engineer Mountain 7.5 minute Latitude 40, Durango Trails
ELEVATION GAIN	2,270 feet
RATING	Difficult
ROUND-TRIP DISTANCE	7.2 miles
ROUND-TRIP TIME	4–6 hours
NEAREST LANDMARK	Coal Bank Pass

COMMENT: Engineer Mountain, a significant landmark in the San Juan Mountains, is visible for many miles as you drive north from Durango. The route to the summit ascends steep lower slopes through alpine forest, then rolling open slopes above timberline before a scramble up the Northeast Ridge to the summit. A hike up any portion of the ridge is worthwhile—the tundra slopes teem with wildflowers in summer—and those who achieve the summit also are treated to panoramas of many San Juan peaks, near and distant, in all directions.

GETTING THERE: From 32nd Street in Durango, drive 33 miles north on U.S. 550 to the summit of Coal Bank Pass. Just north of the pass, turn left at a narrow entrance into a parking lot.

THE ROUTE: Begin your climb on the west side of the parking lot, on the Pass Creek Trail. It gradually ascends around the east side of the first ridge. Stay on the main trail past a stagnant pond and up to a larger pond, at 11,120 feet. On the north side of this ridge hikers often encounter large snow piles on the main trail until mid-June.

Continue upward for 0.75 mile to timberline and the wild-

Engineer Mountain viewed from the slopes of Snowdon Peak.

PHOTO BY JEFF EISELE

flower meadows just above. A beautiful flower display adorns
this area in midsummer, and this is the destination for many
day hikers. As the trail rises to this slope, it intersects the
Engineer Mountain Trail traversing generally in a north-
south direction. To your right is Jura Knob, where this trail
goes and intersects the Colorado Trail to the north. Take a
right, cross a small stream, and pass a trail sign. To your left
and proceeding up the hill begins the "elevator" trail. This
section rises to the red-colored ridge after going past a large
boulder known as "Social Rock" because of the ideal marker
and meeting place it provides.

From here, the trail becomes very steep and is sometimes
covered with snow. Follow the pathways to the left, as there are
many options. Efforts are being made to better define the trail
at this point and slow down the erosion that often results
from people plunge-stepping in the soft dirt on their way
down. Please stay on the more-used portions. The best climbing is near the top of the ridge, where there is a well-worn
trail. As you ascend toward a red ledge overlook, and a higher
white ledge, skirt the outcroppings of rock to the right.

High peaks of the San Juans as seen from the Engineer Mountain summit.

Above the rest point at the white overlook (at 12,000 feet), you are walking on loose plate rock. A trail stays on top of the ridge, or a bit right of it, as you climb toward the crux, which is a short chimney scramble. The rock in this area is generally stable and edgy—providing good traction—but use caution because of the exposure and steepness. Getting out of this chimney area can be done one of three ways: scramble left out of the bottom and climb up, or left, into a gash (very exposed); midway you can find enough cracks and holds to climb on to the upside and scramble right up to the ridge (this is the recommended option used by most climbers); or at the end of the chimney there is a 12-foot up-climb (Class 3-plus), but it is quite airy and hazardous. All of these ways lead to a trail on top of the ridge that continues up to a head-wall. Cross to the left and find the continuation of the trail, which is best followed near the ridge crest or a bit left, all the way to the summit at 12,972 feet. Retrace your steps to return to the trailhead.

10. Grand Turk and Sultan Peaks

BY KERRY HONSINGER

MAPS	Trails Illustrated, Telluride/Silverton/ Ouray/Lake City, Number 141 USGS, Silverton and Snowdon Peak 7.5 minute
ELEVATION GAIN	2,460 feet
RATING	Difficult
ROUND-TRIP DISTANCE	7.5 miles
ROUND-TRIP TIME	4.5–6.5 hours
NEAREST LANDMARK	Molas Pass

COMMENT: Grand Turk and Sultan are the distinctive peaks visible to the west from the town of Silverton. This hike is not technically hard, but both Grand Turk and Sultan rise above 13,000 feet, and the trail passes near the summit of another thirteener, Spencer Peak; thus, the hike earns a "difficult" rating. It is, however, an easy double-thirteener day hike. It does involve route finding, as the trail does not develop until you are well above timberline. The route finding itself is easy, and the lower half of the route is visible from U.S. 550 at Molas Pass.

GETTING THERE: From Durango, drive 40 miles north on U.S. 550, over Coalbank and Molas passes, to the Little Molas Lake turnoff on the west side of the highway. Follow the road into Little Molas Lake and the campground. About 0.75 mile in, the one-way campground loop begins; notice here a short red-soil slope immediately off the roadway to the north. This is the starting point of the hike; you will walk back to this point. Follow the road to the far end of the campground and large parking area.

THE ROUTE: Walk back up the road to the red-soil slope. This access puts you on an old road on a small ridge, minimizing the need to bushwhack in the denser forest. The road turns

The lower part of the route, designated by the red line, is visible from U.S. 550 at Molas Pass, showing the route to the small bowl above the basin between two rock outcroppings. PHOTO BY KERRY HONSINGER

into a trail that eventually runs out. Look north-northwest through the trees for two prominent outcroppings. Head toward the basin between these outcroppings. The terrain will start to steepen dramatically as you approach the benched slopes. These slopes are loaded with wild strawberries in July.

As you work your way up the benched slopes, you will notice white horizontal rock bands on the benches, and the trees will get thinner. Before climbing the last slopes to the basin, work your way east to cross the creek that drains from the basin. It is best to do this before the waterfall. Make your way up the steep slope east of the creek. There are some faint trails through the willows.

Once above the waterfall, you are in the basin, at 11,600 feet. Wind your way through the short sections of willows on faint game trails, staying on the east side of the creek. Look up the basin on the east side and you will see a faint trail that goes up to the saddle. This is the trail to the peaks.

The saddle and ridge to the summit of Sultan, as seen from the Grand Turk summit.

The trail will go through a short section of rocks. Continue on to a saddle. At 12,400 feet, you will reach a small grassy bowl above the saddle. Snow lingers in this area well into July and even August. A point rises 500 feet directly in front of you. Traverse east-northeast around this point until you come to a saddle between this point and 13,087-foot Spencer Peak to the east. The trail continues on the south side of this saddle and traverses the north side of Spencer Peak on scree/talus, but you may choose to go over Spencer's summit.

Grand Turk and Sultan are now visible to the north. Descend about 300 feet to another saddle and veer right to climb Grand Turk. It has many summits, but the first three points up from the saddle are the highest. The third one is marked as the high point, at 13,148 feet.

From Grand Turk, drop down to the saddle to the north and follow the faint climbers' trail up the talus ridge to the summit of Sultan, at 13,368 feet, and a fantastic aerial view of Silverton. Retrace your steps to get back to the trailhead.

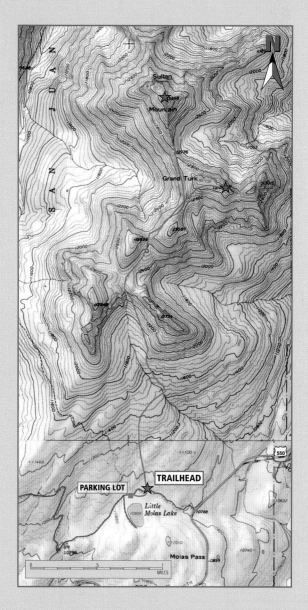

PARKING LOT

TRAILHEAD

Little
Molas Lake

Molas Pass

11. Hesperus Mountain

BY MIKE FRISONI

MAPS	Trails Illustrated, Durango/Cortez, Number 144 USGS, La Plata 7.5 minute Latitude 40, Durango Trails
ELEVATION GAIN	2,470 feet
RATING	Difficult
ROUND-TRIP DISTANCE	3.6 miles (6.6 miles from spur road intersection, where four-wheel-drive is recommended)
ROUND-TRIP TIME	4–7 hours (5.5–8.5 hours from spur road intersection)
NEAREST LANDMARK	Town of Mancos

COMMENT: Hesperus Mountain is the high point of the La Plata Range, rising to an elevation of 13,232 feet. Hesperus is notable as the Diné (Navajo) People's Sacred Mountain of the North, which marks the northern boundary of their traditional homeland. The peak is climbed from the north side of the West Ridge. Accessing the ridge is mostly off-trail and offers an opportunity to test your route-finding skills through evergreen stands, downed trees, dense willows, and Class 3 scrambling up talus slopes.

GETTING THERE: From Durango, go west on U.S. 160 for 27 miles to the junction with Colorado 184 in Mancos. From here, it is 19.8 miles to your driving destination, the Sharkstooth Trailhead, mostly on good paved or gravel roads. Mark this point. Take 184 north 0.3 mile and turn right onto Montezuma County Road 42 at a sign for Mancos State Park and Jackson Lake. At mile 5.5, you enter the San Juan National Forest and the road becomes Forest Service Road 561. The Transfer Campground is at mile 10.0. There are additional roadside camping opportunities farther along the road, except at the trailhead where camping is prohibited. At mile 12.0, turn right onto FS 350 (Spruce Mill Road). A few roads will branch off, but stay on FS 350 until mile

Morning light on Hesperus Mountain.

18.3, then veer right on a spur road marked by a sign for Twin Lakes and Sharkstooth Trailhead. A high-clearance, four-wheel-drive vehicle is recommended beyond this point. Follow the road for 1.5 miles to the trailhead.

THE ROUTE: From the parking area, there are two trailhead signs. The southeast trail goes to Sharkstooth and Centennial peaks. Take the trail that heads south, which is West Mancos Trail No. 621. Follow this trail 0.5 mile to a good log bridge that crosses the North Fork of the West Mancos River. Shortly after the drainage crossing, follow the trail another 0.1 mile through an open avalanche path below the upper face of Hesperus, past a stand of spruce and fir, and to a clearing of dense foliage. You have gone too far if the trail begins to descend. At this point, leave the trail to the south and begin finding your own route through the foliage, timber, and willows, ascending toward the West Ridge. The least difficult path is the transition zone between the timber and the willows.

Above the timber is a grassy slope that leads to a talus field. At 11,270 feet, traverse the talus to the southwest. After a short

The route up pyramid-shaped Hesperus traverses the northwest face to the edge of the right skyline. Centennial, center, and Sharkstooth, left, peaks also are seen in this view of the West Mancos River Valley. PHOTO BY JEFF EISELE

distance, ascend a debris flow heading south and onto a grass and rock slope. This leads to a flat, grassy knoll. A steep slope of loose talus is above this flat area. Use caution as you climb this 200-foot pitch to a large flat bench. Traverse the bench to the southwest and ascend the dirt and rock slope to the top of the ridge, where a cairn-marked trail leads to the summit. The trail follows just below the summit ridge crest on the south side, with occasional scrambling to gain the top of the ridge. The north side of the ridge is quite precipitous.

There is a rock windbreak on the summit that will allow a small group to enjoy views of the San Juan Range and the Abajo and LaSal mountain ranges of southeastern Utah. Several of Colorado's fourteener summits are prominent on the distant skyline.

For the descent, follow the same route, or hike further west down the ridge and descend one of the dirt or grassy slopes to the talus fields below.

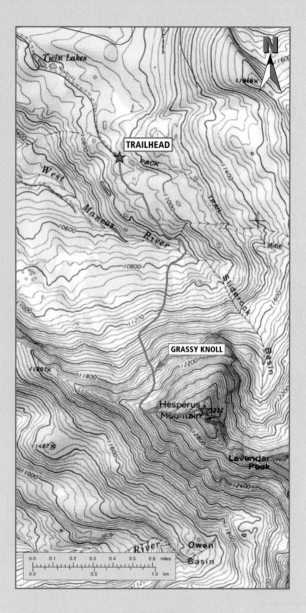

12. Highland Mary and Verde Lakes

BY JEFF EISELE

MAPS	Trails Illustrated, Weminuche Wilderness, Number 140 USGS, Howardsville 7.5 minute Latitude 40, Telluride/Silverton/Ouray
ELEVATION GAIN	1,320 feet to Highland Mary Lakes; 1,450 feet to Verde Lakes; 2,500 feet for Continental Divide Loop
RATING	Moderate–difficult
ROUND-TRIP DISTANCE	4.0 miles to Highland Mary Lakes; 6.0 miles to Verde Lakes; 10.0 miles for Continental Divide Loop
ROUND-TRIP TIME	2–3.5 hours to Highland Mary Lakes; 3.5–5 hours to Verde Lakes; 6–8 hours for Continental Divide Loop
NEAREST LANDMARK	Town of Silverton

COMMENT: This area east of Silverton offers a number of options to visit several alpine lakes above 12,000 feet, with near and distant panoramas of dozens of high peaks of the San Juan Mountains. A round trip to Highland Mary Lakes is a relatively modest effort. The loop, including a section of the Continental Divide Trail, adds several miles and an extra 1,000-plus feet of elevation gain, but it's mostly on gentle terrain.

GETTING THERE: From 32nd Street in Durango, drive 46 miles north on U.S. 550 to Silverton. Drive through town and turn right on San Juan County Road 2. Measure from here. After 2.0 miles, go straight where the road splits. After 4.1 miles, turn right on County Road 4. A sign here directs you to Mine Tours and Stoney Pass; this is the Cunningham Gulch Road. Measure from here now. At 1.7 miles, bear right; do not take the road to Stoney Pass. Bear right again at 3.7 miles, at another split, and cross Cunningham Gulch. The road

Looking north at the middle, left, and upper Highland Mary Lakes on the way to Verde Lakes. PHOTO BY JEFF EISELE

becomes rougher here but, when dry, is passable for most vehicles. At 4.6 miles, turn left on a road leading down to a stream crossing. The trailhead is 0.2 mile ahead. If you don't want to ford the creek in your car, there is space for a few vehicles to park just before the crossing.

THE ROUTE: The trail ascends in a southerly direction. After 0.4 mile, stay straight where a marked stock trail splits off to the left, and cross a creek. After 0.8 mile, a sign marks entry to the Weminuche Wilderness. In the next mile, there are several places where spur trails tempt you to veer right and cross the stream. Be patient and take care to follow the correct path—it might require some trial and error. Eventually, it leads to the base of a rock face; skirt around it on the right side. Just beyond, you will cross a smaller creek, but you will be left (east) of the larger stream.

You'll know you're at the desired stream crossing when you reach a sign marked Highland Marys Trail, pointing you to the other side. The trail now weaves its way through willows,

The author joins the Continental Divide Trail above Verde Lakes.

PHOTO BY JEFF EISELE

another area where staying on course can be difficult. Stay on the right side of the stream and work your way up the slope on that side.

Your route-finding difficulties are now behind you. The trail is easy to follow the rest of the way, regardless of which option you choose. You soon reach the first and smallest of the three Highland Mary Lakes. There are trails circling all of the lakes, and ascending surrounding high points, but the main trail goes around the right side of the lower lake, the left side of the middle lake, and the right side of the upper lake.

You're already surrounded by spectacular vistas in all directions, and this alone is a worthy objective. If you wish to experience more, though, Verde Lakes is another mile south on the main trail. A trip here will bring the magnificent peaks of the Grenadier Range into view to the south. As you near these lakes, you'll see posts on the ridgeline to the southeast. They mark the route of the Continental Divide Trail. This route closely follows the Divide on gentle slopes, and crosses it twice. It roughly parallels your ascent route, about a mile east of it. Eventually, you come to a marked trail junction, where you'll take a connecting trail back to the Highland Mary Lakes Trail, a short distance above the trailhead.

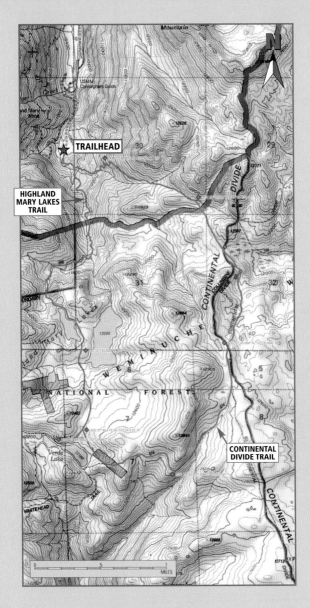

13. Ice Lake Basin Loop

BY JOHN BREGAR

MAPS	Trails Illustrated, Telluride/Silverton/ Ouray/Lake City, Number 141 USGS, Ophir 7.5 minute Latitude 40, Telluride/Silverton/Ouray
ELEVATION GAIN	2,700 feet
RATING	Moderate
ROUND-TRIP DISTANCE	7 miles
ROUND-TRIP TIME	5–7 hours
NEAREST LANDMARK	Town of Silverton

COMMENT: Ice Lake Basin provides alpine tundra at its best, with three large lakes and several smaller ones tucked under spectacular 13,000-foot peaks. Island Lake, northeast of Ice Lake, sits in its own cirque under U.S. Grant Peak. Combining Ice Lake and Island Lake offers a great loop hike. Fuller Lake, the largest in Ice Lake Basin, is an easy mile south of Ice Lake. The tundra affords a wonderful wildflower show from late June through August, and the subalpine flowers along lower portions of the trail are also magnificent.

GETTING THERE: From Durango, drive north on U.S. 550 about 40 miles to Silverton. Continue north on the highway 2 miles and turn left on the road to South Mineral Campground. Take this good dirt road for 4.5 miles to a large parking area on the right, across from the campground.

THE ROUTE: From the parking area, the trail heads west, then begins switchbacking through subalpine forest as it climbs up from the bottom of Mineral Creek Valley and crosses to the west side of the raucous stream tumbling down from Clear Lake to the north. A series of waterfalls will be above you. The trail continues switchbacking, sometimes in forest, sometimes across flower-strewn open slopes, at one point

Upper Ice Lake.

PHOTO BY JOHN BREGAR

passing above the ruins of an old mill.

The trail levels out at 11,400 feet, at the edge of Lower Ice Lake Basin. The high thirteeners come into view for the first time. Look here for a small cairn that marks an indistinct side trail coming in from the north. This unmaintained track leads directly to Island Lake and is part of the loop. You could ascend this side trail, but for purposes of this description, assume you choose to continue west on the main trail.

The trail undulates over gentle terrain teeming with wildflowers. Lower Ice Lake is south of the trail. Ahead looms a headwall of impressive gray cliffs marked by several cascading streams. As the trail approaches the headwall it fords two streams and then begins a rising traverse, aiming for a break in the headwall above a narrow chasm. Beyond the chasm, the trail turns west, then north, and tops another cliff band to enter upper Ice Lake Basin. From here, a short walk brings you to Ice Lake.

Pilot Knob looms over a brilliant blue upper Ice Lake.   PHOTO BY JOHN BREGAR

Over the lake to the west is rugged Pilot Knob. The summit of Golden Horn is obstructed by the enormous buttress of its northeast ridge to the southwest, but further left Fuller and Vermilion peaks are visible. All of these summits make challenging climbs.

You can return the way you came, take a side trip south on a faint track to Fuller Lake, or continue the loop by crossing the outlet of Ice Lake (tricky in high water) and aiming for the dim trail that is visible climbing low on the ridge to the northeast. This trail brings you around the end of the ridge separating Ice Lake Basin from the Island Lake Cirque. After rounding the ridge, the trail becomes harder to follow: aim for the lake, cross the outlet stream, and wander northeast until you find the faint track that you can see coming down from the saddle north of Island Lake.

Follow this trail down a steep, small valley. Eventually, the trail cuts left out of the valley to make a long descending traverse across an open slope before switching back southwest and down to the main Ice Lake Trail at the small cairn you noted on your ascent. Retrace your path back to the trailhead.

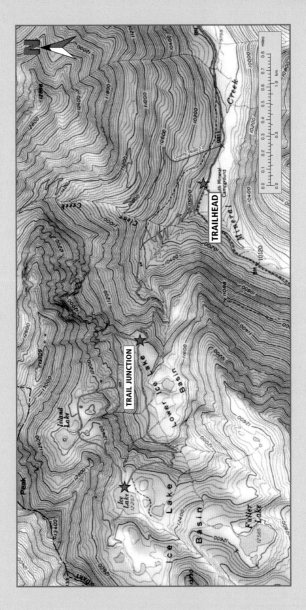

ICE LAKE BASIN LOOP 67

14. Lime Mesa Trail to Mountain View Crest

BY DIANA DONNELLY

MAPS	Trails Illustrated, Weminuche Wilderness, Number 140 USGS, Mountain View Crest 7.5 minute
ELEVATION GAIN	From lower access to Overlook Point, 1,750 feet; from upper access to Overlook Point, 1,500 feet
RATING	Moderate–difficult
ROUND-TRIP DISTANCE	9–10 miles, depending on access and side trips
ROUND-TRIP TIME	6–8 hours
NEAREST LANDMARK	Missionary Ridge

COMMENT: This trail—and an alternate unnamed trail—takes you to one of the most splendid overlooks of the San Juan Mountains, with the option of continuing into the wilderness surrounding those jagged peaks. Starting at timberline, it is a well-defined trail that travels through abundant fields of summer wildflowers and spruce/fir patches among limestone and granite boulders. This trail offers 360-degree views of the mesas to the south, the La Plata Mountains to the west, and the famed peaks of the Weminuche Wilderness to the north and east. This is a wilderness area and dogs must be on a handheld leash.

GETTING THERE: From 32nd Street in Durango, go 8 miles north on U.S. 550 and turn right at the traffic light at Trimble Lane (County Road 252). This road ends after 1 mile at County Road 250, where you turn left. Take this road 3.2 miles and turn right onto Missionary Ridge Road. This gravel road climbs with switchbacks along a shelf that can be slippery. At 11.7 miles, the road forks. Continue straight on FS 682. Travel another 6.5 miles, and turn right on Henderson Lake Road

Diana Donnelly pauses by Dollar Lake, an excellent rest and snack stop.

(FS 081). In 3.8 miles, there is a sharp turn to the right (south) and a parking area on the left with a small trail sign. This is the access to the unnamed, alternate trail at 11,250 feet that is accessible to most vehicles. From here to the end of the road—which is 2.1 miles and the upper trail access— you will need four-wheel-drive. There is a large parking area here and a trail sign.

THE ROUTE: From the lower access, follow the cairns on a beautiful trail along the western side of Lime Mesa to the intersection with the Lime Mesa Trail, at a large cairn, at 11,990 feet. The upper access trail merges from the southeast and looks like an old jeep road.

There is a trail register at the upper access, north of the partly fenced parking area. This trail ascends slightly through fields of wildflowers and small chunks of rock. At 0.8 mile, there is an old sign for the City Reservoir Trail. The Lime Mesa Trail then crosses a large gully before traversing through patchy fields of spruce, fir, and pinkish granite.

Mount Eolus from the Lime Mesa Trail.   PHOTO BY DIANA DONNELLY

There are also chunks of white limestone and granite boulders before the trail arrives at Dollar Lake, at 11,880 feet. This is an excellent rest stop. In 0.5 mile from the lake, you will reach the intersection of the Lime Mesa Trail and the lower, unnamed trail.

Continue your ascent through magnificent alpine tundra and outcroppings of granite and krumholtz. The trail veers to the northeast, then to a Y intersection. Go left here to a saddle, at 12,520 feet. There is an outstanding view here, but if you continue to the left to Overlook Point, 12,998 feet, on Mountain View Crest, there is an even better one. Overlooking Chicago Basin, at your feet are Ruby, Emerald, Pear, and Webb lakes, with the sheer southern faces of Pigeon and Turret peaks directly north and, east of them, the fourteeners Eolus, Sunlight, and Windom. If you continue right (east) from the Y, there is a second saddle and overlook point. Here, the trail also drops down to Ruby and Emerald lakes. Retrace your steps to return to the trailhead.

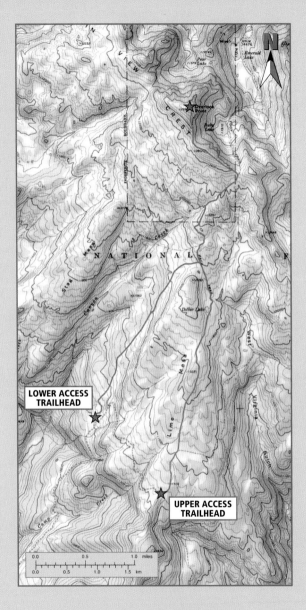

LOWER ACCESS
TRAILHEAD

UPPER ACCESS
TRAILHEAD

15. Lizard Head Trail

BY LASZLO SZUECS

MAPS	Trails Illustrated, Telluride/Silverton/ Ouray/Lake City, Number 141 USGS, Mount Wilson 7.5 minute Latitude 40, Telluride/Silverton/Ouray
ELEVATION GAIN	1,800 feet
RATING	Moderate
ROUND-TRIP DISTANCE	7 miles
ROUND-TRIP TIME	4–6 hours
NEAREST LANDMARK	Lizard Head Pass

COMMENT: This rewarding hike earns you an exceptionally rich set of mountain panoramas. If you are visiting in Durango, the drive to Lizard Head Pass alone is worthwhile. With an early morning start, you can complete this hike and go on to drive the San Juan Skyway loop to Telluride, Ridgeway, Ouray, over Red Mountain Pass to Silverton, and over Molas and Coal Bank passes back to Durango. This loop is one of the most scenic mountain drives in the country.

Best time of the year for this hike is late June through early October. In the early season, the remaining winter snowfields enhance the scenery, and the changing aspen of the late season provide magnificent color. Experienced snowshoers can complete the hike during the winter, but expect some route-finding problems and steep switchbacks.

GETTING THERE: From Durango, take U.S. 160 west to Mancos. At the traffic light, turn right on Colorado 184 and drive 18 miles to a T intersection near Dolores. Turn right on Colorado 145. Follow this highway 53 miles to the trailhead at Lizard Head Pass.

As you head out of Dolores, the first mountain range you will see on your right is the La Platas. You also will enjoy the pastoral tranquility of the Dolores River Valley. At milepost

Lizard Head Peak, center, and Gladstone Peak, as seen from
the Lizard Head Trail.

PHOTO BY LASZLO SZUECS

45 an imposing headwall will appear on the skyline. The top
of the headwall is the ridge that connects Mount Wilson, on
the right, with El Diente; the traverse of this ridge is one of
Colorado's classic climbs.

After passing through the historic mining town of Rico,
the highway climbs into alpine terrain. About 2 miles before
arriving at Lizard Head Pass, the first glimpse of Lizard Head
Peak is on your left. Once at the pass, turn into the large
parking area on your left. There are pit toilets at the trailhead. (NOTE: the USGS topo map shows the trailhead near
Trout Lake; this is obsolete.)

THE ROUTE: The rocky face directly above the trailhead is known
as the Black Face. Its highest point is your destination. The
trail starts from the parking lot and heads northeast across a
meadow. The first 1.5 miles are uneventful; the trail runs
parallel to the highway, through the mixed aspen/spruce
forest until it finds a break in the cliffs above, so it can ascend
to the summit ridge of Black Face.

Vermilion Peak and Golden Horn provide the backdrop for Trout Lake.

PHOTO BY LASZLO SZUECS

The next mile presents a series of switchbacks through the spruce forest. There will be some steep pitches with good footing here. At the Wilson Meadows junction, keep left, continuing on to the Lizard Head Trail.

For the last mile, as the trail follows a gentle ridge, the trees will give way to alpine meadows and gradually a gorgeous 360-degree panorama will unfold. After passing a false summit, you will stand on the highest point of the ridge—the summit of Black Face.

To the west is a close-up view of Lizard Head against a backdrop of the Wilson group. But don't overlook the Sneffels Range to the north, the Ice Lake group in the east, and the La Plata Mountains in the distant south. If you wish to extend your hike, the trail continues for another mile beyond the summit of Black Face to meet the Cross Mountain Trail—you passed its trailhead on the highway 2 miles before Lizard Head Pass. Retrace your steps to your vehicle.

If you choose to drive directly back to Durango, you may want to stop at the Rico Hotel, in the town of Rico, for some delicious apple pie and hot coffee.

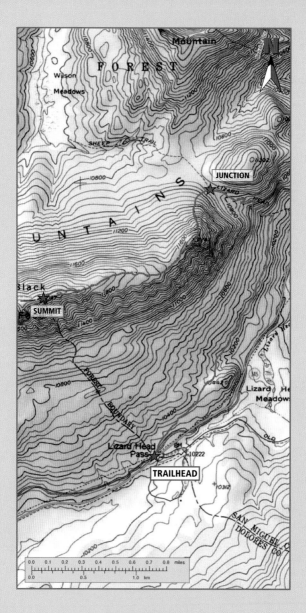

16. Potato Lake Trail

BY JEFF EISELE

MAPS	Trails Illustrated, Weminuche Wilderness, Number 140
	USGS, Engineer Mountain 7.5 minute
	Latitude 40, Durango Trails
ELEVATION GAIN	430 feet
RATING	Easy
ROUND-TRIP DISTANCE	2.3 miles
ROUND-TRIP TIME	1–2 hours
NEAREST LANDMARK	Durango Mountain Resort

COMMENT: The drive time and hiking time are about the same for this hike, but if you're looking for a short, easy hike in the summer, it's a worthwhile escape from Durango for the cooler temperatures at higher elevation. In the fall, it's worth it for the colorful changing of the aspen. This quick getaway offers an easy outing, perfect for families, and could include a picnic lunch or some fishing. You'll also be treated to views of Engineer Mountain to the north, Potato Hill directly above the lake, and the West Needle Mountains to the east. It can easily be done in a half day or less, as a diversion along the way to other destinations in Southwest Colorado. Strong snowshoers and crosscountry skiers can make it a winter destination, but you'll have to walk up Old Lime Creek Road from the highway, making it a 9.3-mile trip—a fairly long distance, but all on open road and good trail.

GETTING THERE: From U.S. 550 and 32nd Street in Durango, drive 27 miles north on U.S. 550. Pass Durango Mountain Resort and Cascade Village, and immediately after a hairpin turn over Cascade Creek, turn right onto Old Lime Creek Road (marked by a sign). Proceed 3.5 miles on the dirt and rocky road to the trailhead that is near the northwest end of a marshy lily pond. There is a parking area on the left side of

Engineer Mountain seen through the trees on the Potato Lake Trail.

the road that is large enough for about four vehicles. If that's full, there is space nearby on the shoulder of the road. The road is rougher for the last mile before reaching the trailhead, but it is drivable by most passenger cars.

THE ROUTE: A sign immediately in front of the parking area marks the trailhead. The route is straightforward as there is a good trail all the way to the lake. The hike begins at an elevation of 9,400 feet and proceeds in a northerly direction, traveling through aspen glades. Along the way, you get glimpses of Engineer Mountain peeking through the trees.

The trail gradually swings to an easterly course through the forest, passing several small ponds along the way. Potato Hill, also known as Spud Mountain, begins to dominate the view to the north. As you near the lake, likewise also known as Spud Lake, the trail turns back to the north and the high peaks of the West Needle Mountains appear to the east. A trail circles the lake, providing numerous places to stop, relax, snack, fish, and soak in the scenery. Return to the trailhead by retracing your footsteps.

Aspen leaves glimmer in autumn sunshine on Potato Lake Trail.   PHOTO BY JEFF EISELE

SIDEBAR HIKING WITH CHILDREN

Hiking with children requires special considerations and advance preparation. Here are some tips:

► Keep children in sight at all times.

► Repeat and repeat again all instructions.

► Choose a hike with modest elevation gains.

► Feed the troops. Begin with a nourishing breakfast. Carry plenty of quick-energy snack foods and offer them frequently.

► Supplement The Ten Essentials with extra snack foods, whistles (in case you and your child become separated), and a book or toy for the drive to and from the trailhead.

► Check your child's temperature. Dress kids in layers and be sure to add or subtract clothing in response to changing weather conditions.

► Teach respect for nature. Enjoy but don't disturb flowers, plants, and animals. Visit park interpretive centers.

► Bring friends. When children travel in groups, the kids motivate each other to go farther and faster. And there's a lot less complaining.

► If young spirits sag, try playing games such as "I Spy" to regain good humor and maintain forward progress up the trail.

► Stop frequently and travel slowly, so you don't have to carry your child later.

Source: John McKinney's *The Hiker's Way: Hike Smart. Live Well. Go Green.* Used by permission of the author and The Trailmaster, Inc.

TRAILHEAD

17. Sand Canyon Loop

BY BERNADETTE TUTHILL

MAPS	USGS, Mariano Wash East; Woods Canyon 7.5 minute Free trail map available at the Anasazi Heritage Center
ELEVATION GAIN	800 feet
RATING	Easy–moderate
ROUND-TRIP DISTANCE	5.25 miles (with longer options)
ROUND-TRIP TIME	2.5–4 hours
NEAREST LANDMARK	Junction of U.S. 160 and Montezuma County Road G (Airport Road)

COMMENT: Sand Canyon is part of the Canyons of the Ancients National Monument (CANM) near the Four Corners in Southwest Colorado. CANM covers 164,000 acres, with more than 20,000 archaeological sites managed by the Bureau of Land Management in Montezuma and Dolores counties. The Anasazi Heritage Center (www.co.blm.gov/ahc) has much information about CANM and Sand Canyon. It is located at 27501 Colorado 184 in Dolores and is well worth a visit.

Sand Canyon is open for hiking, mountain biking, and horseback riding. Dogs are allowed and leashes are recommended. The area is semi-arid with desert canyons and mesas. There are no facilities and no water, so be sure to carry plenty of drinking water. It is a good idea to carry extra water in your vehicle and to fully hydrate from this source before starting out on your hike.

The trails are well defined and marked with cairns. Prehistoric cliff dwellings and ruins can be seen in the alcoves of the walls of the red rock cliffs and canyons. Some ruins are accessible close up. Visitors are asked to be careful not to disturb the archaeological sites or climb on the walls. Pottery shards may be found, but it is illegal to remove or

Hikers make their way down a lower section of the Sand Canyon Trail.

disturb them. CANM should be visited with respect and the Leave No Trace guidelines (see page 97) should be followed.

Cryptobiotic—hidden life—soil is abundant in the area. It looks like bumpy brown or black dirt and contains cyano-bacteria, lichens, and mosses. The soil crust holds water and nutrients and it stabilizes the soil, which in turn prevents erosion—especially from the wind. These soil crusts can take thousands of years to form. One footprint will kill the soil crust, so, in order not to disturb it, please stay on designated trails.

GETTING THERE: From Durango, follow U.S. 160 west for 27 miles, to Colorado 184 in Mancos. (If you are planning to visit the Anasazi Heritage Center before your hike, you can take Colorado 184 north approximately 20 miles.) To get to Sand Canyon, continue west on U.S. 160, and pass through the town of Cortez. On the west side of Cortez, turn right on County Road G, also known as Airport Road. Follow this road for 12.6 miles to the open slickrock parking area on the right.

Numerous spur trails bring visitors up close to the archaeological sites.

You may want to get an early start as the parking lot can become very crowded and much of the surrounding area is privately owned and not available for parking.

THE ROUTE: From the parking lot, hike up the open slickrock toward the monolith and Castle Rock Pueblo behind it. Follow the cairns 0.25 mile to the Sand Canyon/East Rock Creek Trail junction, which is clearly marked. Start the loop in a counterclockwise direction, taking the Sand Canyon Trail to the right. Follow the trail for 1.5 miles to the next trail junction. Explore the many well-marked spurs and viewpoints along the way.

At the 1.5-mile junction, take the 0.75-mile crossover trail to the East Rock Creek Trail. (An option: The Sand Canyon Trail continues north for 5 miles to the ruins of Sand Canyon Pueblo. In about 2.5 miles, you will come to a steep section with 30 switchbacks and 680 feet elevation gain.) The viewpoint near the end of the crossover trail offers views overlooking the East Rock Creek Trail and canyons. See how many ruins you can spot in the canyon walls across the way.

Continue to the next trail junction, marked by another signpost. (Another option: at the junction, bear right on an unmarked trail 0.6 mile to view an arch at the end of the canyon wall; return to the main trail.) Take a left and follow the East Rock Trail 1 mile to the next signpost. At this junction, take a left and follow the trail 1.5 miles back to the trailhead.

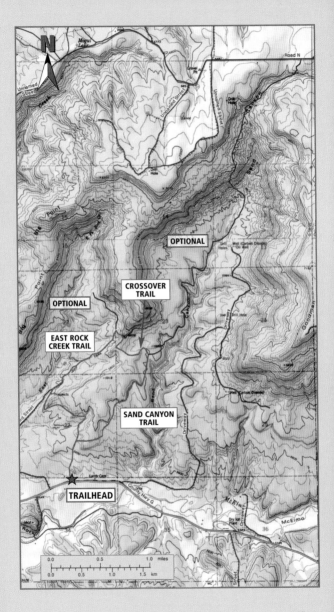

18. Sliderock and Kennebec Trails

BY DOROTHY BREGAR

MAPS	Trails Illustrated, Durango/Cortez, Number 144
	USGS, Monument Hill and Kennebec Pass 7.5 minute
	Latitude 40, Durango Trails
ELEVATION GAIN	1,510 feet
RATING	Easy–moderate
ROUND-TRIP DISTANCE	6 miles
ROUND-TRIP TIME	3–5 hours
NEAREST LANDMARK	City of Durango, Main Avenue and 25th Street

COMMENT: The Sliderock and Kennebec trails follow the portion of the Colorado Trail starting at the intersection with Forest Service Road 171N, ascending the east side of Kennebec Pass, and ending at a four-wheel-drive parking area above La Plata Canyon on the west side of the pass. It's a beautiful hike on a good trail, starting in the trees and ending above timberline, with spectacular skyline views all around. There are many options to extend the hike, adding time, distance, and difficulty. Bring a detailed map along as there are many trails going in different directions. The road to the trailhead is open from late June to late fall, depending on snow conditions. In summer, and until the first snow, the road is passable by most cars, but after the first snows a four-wheel-drive vehicle may be needed.

GETTING THERE: From Main Avenue in Durango, turn west on 25th Street. This will turn into Junction Creek Road as it leaves town. Begin measuring distance when you reach the National Forest boundary at the Junction Creek trailhead, where the pavement ends. At 17.5 miles, look for a dirt road on the left, with a small sign marked 171N. Turn left and go

Cumberland Mountain provides the backdrop for a hiking companion on the Sliderock Trail.   PHOTO BY DEBRA VAN WINEGARDEN

about 0.7 mile, where the Colorado Trail crosses the road. The signs marking the trail are small: you'll first see a sign on the left, then another on the right. There is room for parking on the left side of the road.

THE ROUTE: The trail starts at 10,400 feet, angling up from the road. It rises steadily for 1.5 miles, making a couple of switchbacks through steep meadows and forest, before breaking out into the open with a view of Cumberland Mountain. You'll now be on the Sliderock portion of the trail, which continues up along the side of the valley across an open rocky area for another 0.9 mile to the trail intersection before Kennebec Pass.

Just before you reach the pass, the trail intersects an old mining road. Turn right here and continue another 0.1 mile to the pass. From the pass, continue along the trail another 0.5 mile to the parking area at the head of La Plata Canyon for a fantastic panorama, including Lizard Head and the surrounding mountains to the north. There are signboards

A view of Mount Moss and Lavender Peak from the parking area west of Kennebec Pass.

PHOTO BY JOHN BREGAR

just north of the parking area to help you identify the surrounding peaks.

Other options from the parking area include Taylor Lake or Indian Trail Ridge, which are accessed by continuing west on the Colorado Trail. See the signboard at the parking area for directions. You can also hike up the jeep road from the parking area to a notch in the ridge for a view to the east, or wander down the road to check out the Cumberland Mine ruins.

Another option from the intersection before Kennebec Pass is to bear left, or south, on the mining road and hike 0.25 mile to the Muldoon Mine. A couple of intact buildings remain, including the "Loo with a View." From here, you can look all the way down Junction Creek to Durango and beyond and then take in the spectacular panorama of the high peaks to the northeast, from the Needles to Grizzly Peak. Cumberland Mountain can be climbed by hiking up the grassy east ridge just above the mine, which will take you directly to the summit, a 540-foot ascent. Descending along a faint trail down the northwest ridge to the main trail adds a nice loop. Retrace your steps to return to the trailhead.

19. Smelter Mountain

BY JOHN BREGAR

MAPS	Trails Illustrated, Durango/Cortez, Number 144 USGS, Durango West 7.5 minute
ELEVATION GAIN	1,100 feet to east-end viewpoint; 1,500 feet to summit
RATING	Moderate
ROUND-TRIP DISTANCE	2.0 miles to east-end viewpoint; 4.0 miles to summit
ROUND-TRIP TIME	1.5–2 hours to east-end viewpoint; 2.5–3.5 hours to summit
NEAREST LANDMARK	City of Durango

COMMENT: Named for the old smelter—first lead, then later vanadium and uranium—that used to lie at its base along the Animas River, Smelter Mountain looms over the southwest side of Durango. The summit ridge affords views of Durango's downtown district and the southern terminus of the Durango & Silverton Narrow Gauge Railroad.

The route up the southeast ridge and along the summit ridge is a pleasant hike through a piñon and juniper woodland with an occasional ponderosa pine and colorful wildflowers. The flowers begin blooming in April, and as the early species fade, others follow, often into October.

Many bird species make their home on the mountain. Be on the lookout for scrub and piñon jays, black-capped and mountain chickadees, juniper titmouse, bushtits, rock and Bewick's wrens, spotted towhees, Virginia warblers, lazuli buntings, and many other bird species that make their home on the mountain. Mule deer are frequent, and occasionally, mountain lion tracks can be found.

The trek to the easternmost high point is a worthy objective by itself, but if you want to stand on the highest

Smelter Mountain as seen from the city of Durango.

point, the summit ridge runs west for another mile to the actual 7,725-foot summit.

Smelter Mountain can be hiked in winter snow (although it may be easier with snowshoes) because it is popular with local hikers and a trail is usually compacted soon after every snowfall.

GETTING THERE: From the intersection of U.S. 160 and U.S. 550 in Durango, go south on the combined routes for a bit over 1 mile to a traffic light at Frontage Road. Turn right, and immediately after the road bends left, turn right on County Road 211 and then, within 100 yards, turn right again onto the road to the Durango Pumping Station. Go another 50 yards and find a hikers' parking lot on the left.

THE ROUTE: From the parking lot, find an informal trail down to the ephemeral stream to the north, at the mouth of a small canyon, and climb up the other side to a power line support tower. Here, the trail turns west and is steep and rough for about 100 yards—you may want to use your hands for balance

The Durango Tech Center, at the feet of the La Plata Mountains, seen from near the east-end high point. PHOTO BY JEFF EISELE

in a couple of spots. Continue upward on gentler terrain, and the trail eventually slips to the west side of the ridge.

About 1 mile, and 1,100 vertical feet from the parking lot, the trail tops the east end of the summit ridge. Here, on the first bump a hundred yards or so east of some communication towers, is a great spot to pause and admire the spectacular view. The high peaks of the La Plata Range loom to the northwest. Durango lies at your feet, and you can admire the Animas River Valley and high peaks of the San Juans to the north. During warmer months, turkey vultures and violet-green swallows soar over this spot, as do red-tailed hawks and an occasional golden eagle at any time of year.

A dirt service road leads to the summit another mile west. The road offers mostly a gentle walk as it goes up and down around several groups of communication towers. A thin forest of Douglas fir clings to the steep north slopes. The main road tends to stay to the left, and is gentler, while various service roads are steeper and stay right, closer to the ridge crest. As you near the west end of the mountain, the main road begins to descend to the south, so to stand on the summit you will need to take a service road to the right. Retrace your steps to return to the trailhead.

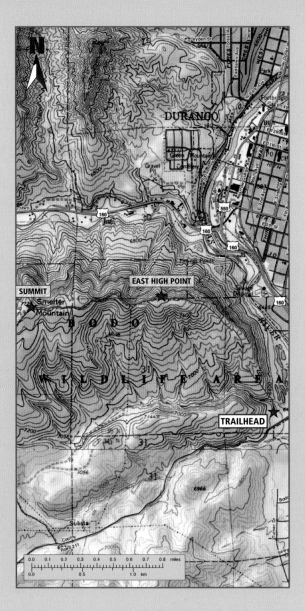

20. Tomahawk Basin and Diorite Peak

BY JEFF EISELE AND CHIP TUTHILL

MAPS	Trails Illustrated, Durango/Cortez, Number 144 USGS, La Plata 7.5 minute Latitude 40, Durango Trails
ELEVATION GAIN	2,900 feet (2,000 feet from Tomahawk Mill; 3,350 feet from Lewis Creek Road)
RATING	Moderate–difficult
ROUND-TRIP DISTANCE	6 miles (or 3.0 miles from Tomahawk Mill; 8.6 miles from Lewis Creek Road)
ROUND-TRIP TIME	3.5–5 hours (or 2–3 hours from Tomahawk Mill; 5–7 hours from Lewis Creek Road)
NEAREST LANDMARK	Intersection of U.S. 160 and Colorado 140

COMMENT: This hike passes the remains of numerous mining sites, starting with the Tomahawk Mill, at 10,760 feet, and extending to a site not far below the 12,761-foot summit of Diorite Peak. The summit provides a great vantage point from which to view the six highest peaks of the La Plata Range—Spiller, Babcock, Lavender, and Centennial peaks, Mount Moss and Hesperus Mountain, all over 13,000 feet—immediately to the west. Diorite is the range's seventh-highest peak.

Much of the structure of the Tomahawk Mill, in particular, remains. However, for your safety and for the protection of the mill and other mine sites, do not enter these or remove any artifacts.

The Tomahawk was a 20-stamp amalgamation mill. Gold ore-bearing rock was reduced to slimes in the stamp batter. Next, mercury was added to the slimes, which were then collected on copper-coated trays. This mix of mercury and gold, called an amalgam, was collected for retorting—a process to vaporize the mercury. The retort sponge was then

Approaching the Tomahawk Mill site on the four-wheel-drive road.

heated in a melting furnace. Additional fluxes were added to separate impurities. These pieces of semi-purified "dore" were collected and cast into bullion.

GETTING THERE: From Durango, take U.S. 160 west 10 miles— 0.5 mile past the intersection of U.S. 160 and Colorado 142— and turn right on La Plata Canyon Road (County Road 124). The road is paved for the first 4.6 miles. After it turns to gravel, you'll pass several campgrounds. The road becomes rougher after 8.5 miles, and those without four-wheel-drive vehicles may want to park at 9.3 miles, where the Lewis Creek Road bears down to the stream to the right. (The road is not marked with a name, but there is a signpost with a numbered address.) With care, two-wheel-drive vehicles with good clearance can proceed. The Tomahawk Basin four-wheel-drive road is a hard left at 10.6 miles. At an elevation of 9,900 feet, this is the designated start of the hike. Four-wheel-drive vehicles can proceed all the way to the mill, about 1.5 miles from this point.

The highest peaks of the La Plata Range viewed from the summit of Diorite Peak.

PHOTO BY JEFF EISELE

THE ROUTE: The 1.5-mile hike up the Tomahawk Basin Road ascends the southwest side of Diorite Peak 860 feet to the mill site, at an elevation of 10,760 feet. Continue hiking up the old double-track mining road, which ascends about 600 feet, via switchbacks through talus slopes, passing near the Little Katie Mine along the way. Spectacular views of the basin and the high western La Platas—Babcock and Spiller first, then Moss, Lavender, and Centennial—emerge as you proceed up the basin.

At 11,350 feet, the route begins to make a more direct assault up Diorite's southwest slopes to an east-west ridge extending from Diorite to Mount Moss. As you climb this slope, you'll pass more mine sites. You'll likely see and hear marmots and pikas, some making homes among the rock foundations of the old mining sites.

Once you reach the ridge, Diorite's summit appears. Skirt around the southeast side of some rock spires to the final 300-foot climb to the summit and the awesome views of the western La Platas—including its monarch, Hesperus, which finally peeks over Lavender and Moss—and Silver Mountain and Lewis Mountain to the east and the San Juans on the northern horizon. Retrace your steps to return to the trailhead.

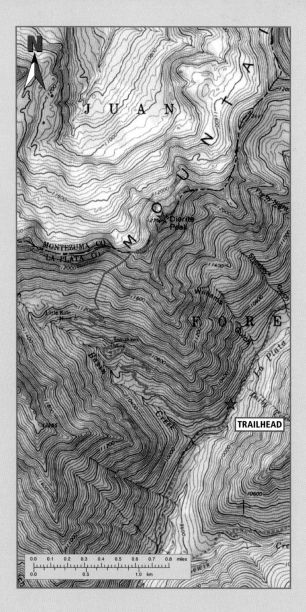

TRAILHEAD

U.S. DEPARTMENT OF THE INTERIOR
Bureau of Land Management

Canyons of
the Ancients
NATIONAL MONUMENT

Castle Rock Monolith frames a sign at the trailhead of the Sand
Canyon Loop hike.   PHOTO BY BERNADETTE TUTHILL

LEAVE NO TRACE

Leave No Trace (LNT) is a national and international program designed to assist outdoor enthusiasts with decisions on reducing their impacts when they hike, camp, picnic, snowshoe, run, bike, hunt, paddle, ride horses, fish, ski, or climb. The program strives to educate all those who enjoy the outdoors about the nature of their recreational impacts as well as techniques to prevent and minimize such impacts.

Below is a list of the Leave No Trace principles. For more information and to get involved, visit the LNT website at www.lnt.org.

Plan Ahead and Prepare

- ► Know the regulations and special concerns for the area you'll visit.
- ► Prepare for extreme weather, hazards, and emergencies.
- ► Schedule your trip to avoid times of high use.
- ► Travel in small groups when possible. Consider splitting larger groups into smaller ones. (On the other hand, solo hiking is considered unnecessarily dangerous, and CMC recommends at least four persons per group.)
- ► Repackage food to minimize waste.
- ► Use a map and compass to eliminate the use of marking paint, rock cairns, or flagging.

Travel and Camp on Durable Surfaces

- ► Durable surfaces include established trails and campsites, rock, gravel, dry grasses, or snow.
- ► Protect riparian areas by camping at least 200 feet from lakes and streams.

The "Loo with a View" at the Muldoon Mine on the Sliderock and Kennebec Trails hike.   PHOTO BY JOHN BREGAR

► Good campsites are found, not made. Altering a site is not necessary.

► In popular areas:
  • Concentrate use on existing trails and campsites.
  • Walk single file in the middle of the trail, even when wet or muddy.
  • Keep campsites small. Focus activity in areas where vegetation is absent.

► In pristine areas:
  • Disperse use to prevent the creation of campsites and trails.
  • Avoid places where impacts are just beginning.
  • In order to not create new trails, do not walk single file— spread out.

Dispose of Waste Properly

- ► Pack it in; pack it out. Inspect your campsite and rest areas for trash or spilled foods. Pack out all trash, leftover food, and litter. Don't hesitate to pack out trash that others have left behind.

- ► Deposit solid human waste in catholes dug 6 to 8 inches deep at least 200 feet from water, camp, and trails. Cover and disguise the cathole when finished.

- ► Pack out toilet paper and hygiene products.

- ► To wash yourself or your dishes, carry water 200 feet away from streams or lakes and use small amounts of biodegradable soap. Scatter strained dishwater.

Leave What You Find

- ► Preserve the past: examine, but do not touch, cultural or historic structures and artifacts.

- ► Leave rocks, plants, and other natural objects as you find them.

- ► Avoid introducing or transporting non-native species.

- ► Do not build structures or furniture, or dig trenches.

Minimize Campfire Impacts

- ► Campfires can cause lasting impacts to the backcountry. Use a lightweight stove for cooking and enjoy a candle lantern for light.

- ► Where fires are permitted, use established fire rings, fire pans, or mound fires.

- ► Keep fires small. Only use sticks from the ground that can be broken by hand.

- ► Burn all wood and coals to ash, put out campfires completely, then scatter cool, wet ashes.

The wide, deep chasm of Mill Creek stretches out below the trail on the Columbine Lake hike. PHOTO BY JEFF EISELE

Respect Wildlife

► Observe wildlife from a distance. Do not follow or approach them.

► Never feed animals. Feeding wildlife damages their health, alters natural behaviors, and exposes them to predators and other dangers.

► Protect wildlife and your food by storing rations and trash securely.

► Control pets at all times, or leave them at home. Dogs must be kept on a handheld leash in designated wilderness areas and wilderness travel zones.

► Avoid wildlife during sensitive times: mating, nesting, raising young, or winter.

Be Considerate of Other Visitors

► Respect other visitors and protect the quality of their experience.

► Be courteous. Yield to other users on the trail.

► Take breaks and set up camp away from trails and other visitors.

► Let nature's sounds prevail. Avoid loud voices and noises.

ABOUT THE AUTHOR

 Jeff Eisele is a veteran journalist with more than 25 years' experience as a reporter, editor, and newsroom manager with the *Sky-Hi News* in Granby, Colo.; *The Daily Press* in Paso Robles, Calif.; *The Desert Sun* in Palm Springs, Calif.; *The Fort Collins Coloradoan*, and *The Durango Herald*.

Jeff grew up in the Denver suburbs and enjoyed a variety of outdoor activities in Colorado's mountains as a youth. Returning to Colorado in 1996 after spending 11 years in California, his passion for hiking and climbing took off a couple years later as he prepared to fulfill a desire he had as a teenager—to climb Longs Peak. He started small, first climbing 7,255-foot Horsetooth Rock west of Fort Collins in the spring, and gradually worked his way up to higher-elevation summits. By the end of fall 1998, he had climbed his first 11 fourteeners—Longs Peak among them—and was hooked.

Jeff joined the Colorado Mountain Club in 2002 to meet others who shared his passion and explore new mountain destinations. A year later, he took the Fort Collins Group's Basic Mountaineering Course (BMC), providing him with the skills to climb more difficult routes on more difficult mountains. He since has served as a junior instructor for BMC as well as activities director and newsletter co-editor for the Fort Collins Group. He also was a contributing writer and photographer for *The Best Fort Collins Hikes*. He now claims 44 fourteener summits and 57 centennials—the highest 100 peaks in Colorado.

In 2008, Jeff moved to Durango, where he is weekend editor at the *Herald*. He spends as much time as he can exploring the mountain and desert trails of the Four Corners. He is the proud father of two college-age daughters, Erin and Emily.

A hiker admires the view from near the east-end high point on the Smelter Mountain hike.